P9-CMS-684

TO: Aunt Lou
LOVE: Tammy

Mothers
Are Special

COMPILED BY
LUCY MEAD

GRAMERCY BOOKS
NEW YORK

Copyright © 2000 by Random House Value Publishing

All rights reserved under International and Pan-American Conventions.

No part of this book may be reproduced or transmitted in any form or by any means, electronic or mechanical including photocopying, recording, or by any information storage and retrieval system, without permission in writing from the publisher.

This 2005 edition is published by Gramercy Books, an imprint of Random House Value Publishing, a division of Random House, Inc., New York.

Gramercy is a registered trademark and the colophon is a trademark of Random House, Inc.

Random House
New York • Toronto • London • Sydney • Auckland
www.randomhouse.com

Interior design: Karen Ocker Design, New York

Printed and bound in Singapore

A catalog record for this title is available from the Library of Congress.

ISBN 0-517-22483-6

10 9 8 7 6 5 4 3

Mothers
Are Special

If you bungle raising your children, I don't think
whatever else you do well matters very much.

JACQUELINE KENNEDY ONASSIS

It wasn't long before he [my father] and his brother, Sarge,
opened up their own garage. Their mother immediately
insisted that the rest of the family move into the adjacent
house....so she could be sure the boys had hot meals.
Now, that's a real Italian mother for you.

ANNETTE FUNICELLO

A man who has been the indisputable favorite of his
mother keeps for life the feeling of a conqueror, that confi-
dence of success that often induces real success.

SIGMUND FREUD

There never was a woman like her. She was gentle as a dove and brave as a lioness...The memory of my mother and her teachings were, after all, the only capital I had to start life with, and on that capital I have made my way.

ANDREW JACKSON

Mothers, food, love, and career,
the four major guilt groups.

CATHY GUISEWITE

God could not be everything
and therefore he made mothers.

JEWISH PROVERB

My mother was the most beautiful woman I ever saw. All I am I owe to my mother. I attribute all my success in life to the moral, intellectual and physical education I received from her.

GEORGE WASHINGTON

I was born because my mother
needed a fourth for meals.

BEATRICE LILLIE, *actress*

Experts say you should never hit your children in anger.
When is a good time? When you're feeling festive?

ROSEANNE BARR

I was determined that no daughter of mine was going to have to go through the agony of being afraid to say what she had on her mind...Just because she was a girl didn't mean she should be limited...

DOROTHY RODHAM, *mother of Hillary Clinton*

What my mother believed about cooking
is that if you worked hard and prospered,
someone else would do it for you.

NORA EPHRON

The best way to keep children at home is to make the home atmosphere pleasant—and let the air out of their tires.

DOROTHY PARKER

...all I saw was Sandra Dee and Doris Day,
and I knew I would never look like either of them...
My mom used to tell me to be glad I was different.
She said, "your day will come."

CHER

Every mother's day my mom and I spend the day alone
together. We go to a secret place in the woods that she
chooses—it's her special day—and we hunt mushrooms,
pick wildflowers, look for deer, and do all the outdoor
things that my mom loves so much. It's my favorite mother-
daughter day.

SAMANTHA, AGE 9 1/2

"How has your perspective changed since you've become a mother?

"Now I really want to stay alive forever. I mean, she comes first. That's how it's changed my perspective—and everything else falls behind it. It's changed my priorities, and I'm sure it will affect every decision I make until I die."

MADONNA

There never was child so lovely but
his mother was glad to get him asleep.

RALPH WALDO EMERSON

✿ ✿ ✿

A mother understands what a child does not say.

OLD SAYING

The funniest thing my mother ever did was roast a
Thanksgiving turkey with its insides— in their plastic bag—
still in the bird. As you might have guessed, my mother did
not have a large following as a dinner party hostess.

ROSALIE, AGE 52

To describe my mother would be to
write about a hurricane in its perfect power.

MAYA ANGELOU

There are just times when you have to be there. Your kids
are the most important thing. I don't want to read in *People*
magazine when I'm sixty that I never saw my children and
they hate me. Wouldn't that be awful?

TRACEY ULLMAN

12

A mother's arms are made of tenderness
and children sleep soundly in them.

VICTOR HUGO

❁ ❁ ❁

Working mother is a misnomer. . . . It implies that any
mother without a definite career is indolently not working, lolling around eating bon-bons, reading novels, and
watching soap operas. But the word "mother" is already a
synonym for some of the hardest, most demanding work
ever shouldered by any human.

LIZ SMITH

❁ ❁ ❁

Mother is the name for God in the
lips and hearts of children.

WILLIAM PEACE THACKERAY

My mother made a brilliant impression
upon my childhood life. She shone for me like
the evening star—I loved her dearly…

WINSTON CHURCHILL

Beautiful as seemed Mamma's face, it became
incomparably more lovely when she smiled, and
seemed to enliven everything about her.

LEO TOLSTOY

As for the mother, her very name stands for loving
unselfishness and self-abnegation and in any society fit to
exist, it is fraught with associations which render it holy.

THEODORE ROOSEVELT

My mother had a great deal of trouble
with me, but I think she enjoyed it.

MARK TWAIN

Mothers are like water; they help you grow.
Without them you would wither and die; but
too much water will always kill a flower.

CASSIE, AGE 16

All the philosophy in our house is not in the study. A good
deal is in the kitchen, where a fine old lady thinks high
thoughts and does good deeds while she cooks and scrubs.

LOUISA MAY ALCOTT

And the life of a working mother who lives without the
constant presence and support of the father of her children
is three times harder than that of any man I have ever met.

GOLDA MEIR

If evolution really works, how
come mothers only have two hands?

MILTON BERLE

Always be nice to your children because they are
the ones who will choose your rest home.

PHYLLIS DILLER

In all my efforts to learn to read, my mother shared fully my ambition and sympathized with me and aided me in every way she could. If I have done anything in life worth attention, I feel sure that I inherited the disposition from my mother.

BOOKER T. WASHINGTON

No painter's brush, nor poet's pen
In justice to her fame
Has ever reached half high enough
To write a mother's name.

ANONYMOUS

A picture memory brings to me;
I look across the years and see
Myself beside my mother's knee.
I feel her gentle hand restrain
My selfish moods, and know again
A child's blind sense of wrong and pain.
But wiser now,
a man gray grown,
My childhood's needs are better known.
My mother's chastening love I own.

JOHN GREENLEAF WHITTIER

The mother's heart is the child's schoolroom.

HENRY WARD BEECHER

All that I am or ever hope to be,
I owe to my angel Mother.

ABRAHAM LINCOLN

The heart of a mother is a deep abyss at the bottom
of which you will always find forgiveness.

HONORE DE BALZAC

Of all the rights of women,
the greatest is to be a mother.

LIN YUTANG, *Chinese Writer, author of My Country and My People*

19

People came over to my parents' house after the screening [of Mean Streets]. Everyone was saying how much they liked the film. And my mother said, "I just want you to know, we never use that word in the house!"

MARTIN SCORSESE

By and large, mothers and housewives are the only workers who do not have regular time off. They are the vacationless class.

ANNE MORROW LINDBERGH

Never lend your car to anyone to whom you have given birth.

ERMA BOMBECK

Arthur: "It's at times like this I wish I'd listened to my mother."
Ford: "Why, what did she say?"
Arthur: "I don't know, I never listened."

DOUGLAS ADAMS, *The Hitchhiker's Guide to the Galaxy*

Because I feel that in the heavens above
The angels, whispering one to another,
Can find among their burning terms of love,
None so devotional as that of "Mother,"
Therefore by that dear name I have long called you,
You who are more than mother unto me

EDGAR ALLAN POE, *To My Mother*

After ecstasy, the laundry.

ZEN SAYING

When my mother had to get dinner for eight she'd just make enough for sixteen and only serve half.

GRACIE ALLEN, *Comedienne*

It seems to me that my mother was the most splendid woman I ever knew....I have met a lot of people knocking around the world since, but I have never met a more thoroughly refined woman than my mother. If I have amounted to anything, it will be due to her.

CHARLIE CHAPLIN

I love my mom like a Heshey [sic] kiss.

LARA, AGE 5

No matter how old a mother is
she watches her middle-aged children
for signs of improvement.

FLORIDA SCOTT-MAXWELL, *American writer
and psychologist (from The Measure of My Days)*

There are only two things a child will share willingly—
communicable diseases and his mother's age.

BENJAMIN SPOCK

…Unseen, unfelt, she extends her influence far and wide.
She is forming the future patriot, statesman, or enemy of his
country; more than this she is sowing the seeds of virtue or
vice, which will fit him for Heaven, or for eternal misery.
Noble, sublime, is the task of the American mother…

The Ladies' Companion, 1840

Separate from my boundaries, I had
known before that he had and would
have a life beyond being my son….
He was three and I was nineteen,
and never again would I think of him
as a beautiful appendage of myself.

MAYA ANGELOU

Let me not forget that I am the daughter of a woman… who herself never ceased to flower, untiringly, during three quarters of a century.

COLETTE

❀ ❀ ❀

The tie which links mother and child
is of such pure and immaculate strength
as to be never violated.

WASHINGTON IRVING

Ah, lucky girls who grew up in the shelter of a mother's love—a mother who knows how to contrive opportunities without conceding favors, how to take advantage of propinquity without allowing appetite to be dulled by habit.

EDITH WHARTON

If a mother respects both herself and her child
from his very first day onward, she will never
need to teach him respect for others.

ALICE MILLER

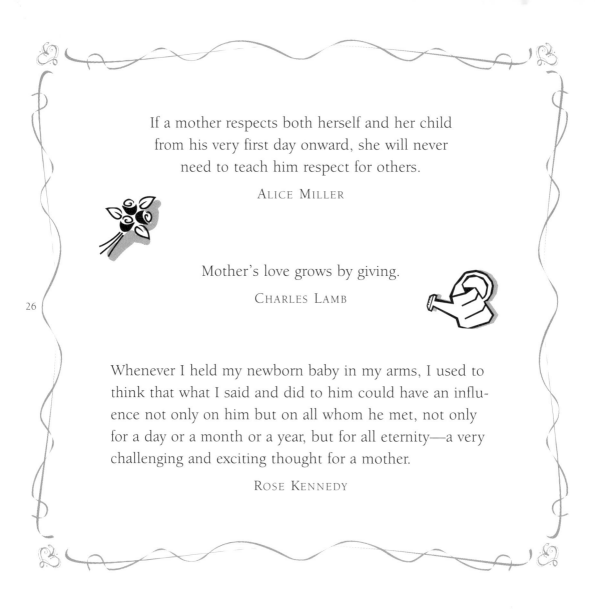

Mother's love grows by giving.

CHARLES LAMB

Whenever I held my newborn baby in my arms, I used to
think that what I said and did to him could have an influence not only on him but on all whom he met, not only
for a day or a month or a year, but for all eternity—a very
challenging and exciting thought for a mother.

ROSE KENNEDY

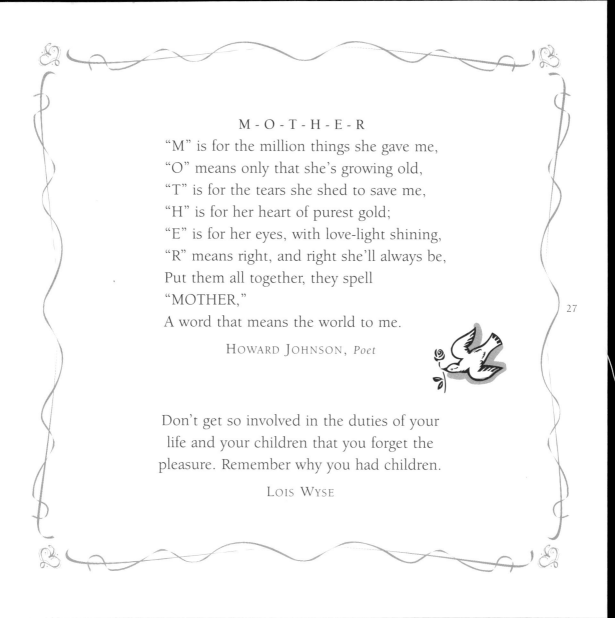

M - O - T - H - E - R

"M" is for the million things she gave me,
"O" means only that she's growing old,
"T" is for the tears she shed to save me,
"H" is for her heart of purest gold;
"E" is for her eyes, with love-light shining,
"R" means right, and right she'll always be,
Put them all together, they spell
"MOTHER,"
A word that means the world to me.

HOWARD JOHNSON, *Poet*

Don't get so involved in the duties of your
life and your children that you forget the
pleasure. Remember why you had children.

LOIS WYSE

My mother always said,
"Even a blind pig finds an acorn now and then."

RON, AGE 46

My mother and all three of my sisters all managed
to have both career and family, to have their own
interests and enthusiasms. I suppose that's the way
I expect women to be and, if they aren't like that,
I feel there's a dimension missing.

JOHN TRAVOLTA

My mother had a slender, small body, but a large
heart—a heart so large that everybody's joys found
welcome in it, and hospitable accommodation.

MARK TWAIN

My mom instilled a lot of values about
living in me—what's right and what's wrong.
She made me feel safe about the world.

DENNIS QUAID

Women know
The way to rear up children (to be just)
They know a simple, merry, tender knack
Of tying sashes, fitting baby-shoes,
And stringing pretty words that make no sense,
And kissing full sense into empty words.

ELIZABETH BARRETT BROWNING

She's [my mother's] mainly interested in basic things like eating and breathing. She's a very secure person, sort of like, uh, normal.

BARBRA STREISAND

My mother said to me, "If you become a soldier you'll be a general; if you become a monk you'll end up as the pope." Instead, I became a painter and wound up as Picasso.

PABLO PICASSO

All women become like their mothers. That is their tragedy. No man does. That's his.

OSCAR WILDE, *The Importance of Being Earnest*

No one in the world can take the place of
your mother. Right or wrong, from her viewpoint
you are always right. She may scold you for little
things, but never for the big ones.

HARRY TRUMAN

Once when my son was about 2-1/2 years old, I called
home around 7 P.M. to tell the nanny I was going to be
late and she should put him to bed. He got on the phone
to talk to me.

"Nicky," I said. "Mommy's stuck at work."

There was along pause, and then he said with worry in
his voice, "Stuck?"

I realized he was thinking of glue, and perhaps imagining
that I was pasted to my desk and would be there forever.

MARY, AGE 35

Mothers all want their sons to grow up
to be president, but they don't want them
to become politicians in the process.

JOHN FITZGERALD KENNEDY

I tend to kind of isolate myself and I'm not a very social
being, so I can drive myself crazy with my own thoughts.
I think that when you become a parent, you just don't
have time for that kind of narcissism, and your whole perspective shifts in a very healthy way.

MICHELLE PFEIFFER

After my little girl was born, I spent so much time by myself, feeding and rocking her and watching her sleep, that I was putting on the television just to hear an adult voice. But what I found wasn't even a quarter good. So I took the televisions away. Now, in the morning, instead of turning on the *Today* show, I give my full attention to the children. And instead of watching *Barney*, they give their full attention to me.

LINDA RONSTADT

The people in the Navy look on motherhood
as being compatible with being a woman.

REAR ADMIRAL JAMES R. HOGG

My two children have opened up love in me I didn't
know I had. They have expanded my world and made it
full of possibilities—because they see through new eyes
and open my eyes, and because their lives will go many
directions mine did not, and they will take me along for
part of their journey.

Karen, age 43

❦ ❦ ❦

I have heard a lot of people, especially people who have
been exposed to military cooking, make disparaging
remarks about creamed chipped beef, but my mom's was
excellent. Perhaps this was because she never served in
the military.

Dave Barry

…the commercial Mother's Day seems designed to salute
a mother who is an endangered species, if not an outright
fraud. A mother who is pink instead of fuchsia…who
bakes cookies and never cheats with the microwave…
who does not swear or scream, who wears an apron and
a patient smile.

ANNA QUINDLEN

The price of [a mother] holding down
two demanding occupations, one at
home and the other away, is high:
constant fatigue and overloaded circuits.

DANIELS & WEINGARTEN,
Sooner or Later; The Timing of Parenthood in Adult Lives

Mama always said life was like a
box a chocolates, never know
what you're gonna get.

FORREST GUMP

Mother has made up her mind: she won't meddle. In the
first place, what does she know? She is, after all, just an
old-fashioned woman. Nowadays the eggs consider them-
selves wiser than the hens. In the second place, would he
even listen to her? And what would she gain if her son, by
disobeying his mother and doing exactly the opposite of
what she said, became guilty thereby of a grievous sin?

CHAIM GRADE, *My Mother's Sabbath Days*

You're not famous until my
mother has heard of you.

JAY LENO

"Have you done your homework?" my mother would ask.
"I'll do it later."
"You will do it now. I don't want you winding up on the
third shift [at the local textile plant]."

... I never could figure how failing to read three chapters in
my geography book about the various sorts of vegetables to
be found in a tropical rain forest had anything to do with
facing life as a mill hand. But with enough guilt and fear as
catalyst, you can read anything...

LEWIS GRIZZARD

The little fawn understood not one of the many songs and
calls, not a word of the conversations. ...Nor did he heed
any of the odors which blew through the woods. He only
heard the soft licking against his coat that washed him and
warmed him and kissed him. And he smelled nothing but
his mother's body near him. She smelled good to him
and, snuggling closer to her, he hunted eagerly around
and found nourishment for his life.

FELIX SALTEN, *Bambi*

Grown don't mean nothing to a mother.
A child is a child. They get bigger, older,
but grown. In my heart it don't mean a thing.

TONI MORRISON

I don't think either my husband or I knew what we were getting into when we had children. I don't think you can. People who are already parents will tell you that you won't believe what it will do to your life. And you sort of nod and go, "Uh, huh." But you don't know.

CINDY, AGE 30

Arnold: "I've taught myself how to cook, sew, fix plumbing and even give myself a pat on the back when necessary. The only thing I need from anyone is love and respect and anyone who can't give me that has no place in my life."

The Mother: "You're throwing me out!?!?"

FROM *Torch Song Trilogy*

… the end of the day… usually finds me sitting in the old rocker, shawl over my shoulders… knitting and purling to my heart's content. I've spent hours in therapy warding off the fear that I would eventually turn into my mother. Whoever thought that I'd actually turn into my grandmother?

ELLEN BYRON, *Playwright*

The older I get, the more of my mother I see in myself. The more opposite my life and my thinking grow from hers, the more of her I hear in my voice, see in my facial expression…To say her image is not still a touchstone in my life—would be another lie.

NANCY FRIDAY, *My Mother My Self*

I think, at a child's birth, if a mother could
ask a fairy godmother to endow it with the most
useful gift, that gift would be curiosity.

ELEANOR ROOSEVELT

Today is Mother's Day, and the room-service waiter at the
hotel is bringing my breakfast....Any of the other 364 days
of the year would be a wonderful time for a woman with
small children to have a morning of peace and quiet. But
solitary splendor on this day is like being a book with no
reader. It raises that age-old question: If a mother screams
in the forest and there are no children to hear it, is there
any sound?

ANNA QUINDLEN, *Thinking Out Loud*

A Freudian slip is when you mean
one thing and say your mother.

ANONYMOUS

But Helen [my mother] looks as though she's
about to start crying. Her eyes redden; her face
whitens...."A lot of crap!" She takes a drink
of her tea. "Who do you think you are, you can
lie to your mother like that?....You are daughter.
Daughter. Do you remember what is a daughter?"

GISH JEN, *Mona in the Promised Land*

Mother is Special:
She's always there for you.
She's very protective.
She lets you wear her special jewelry.
She teaches you about the world.
She tells you the truth.
She hugs you.
She clears the table when you forget.

ISABEL, AGE 13

❀ ❀ ❀

If I had one wish for my children,
it would be that each of them would reach
for goals that have meaning for them as individuals.

LILLIAN CARTER, *mother of President Jimmy Carter*

My mother, religious-negro,
proud of having waded through a
storm, is, very obviously a sturdy
bridge that I have crossed over one.

TONI BAMBARA, *author of Gorilla, My Love*

I know how to do anything—I'm a mom.

ROSEANNE BARR

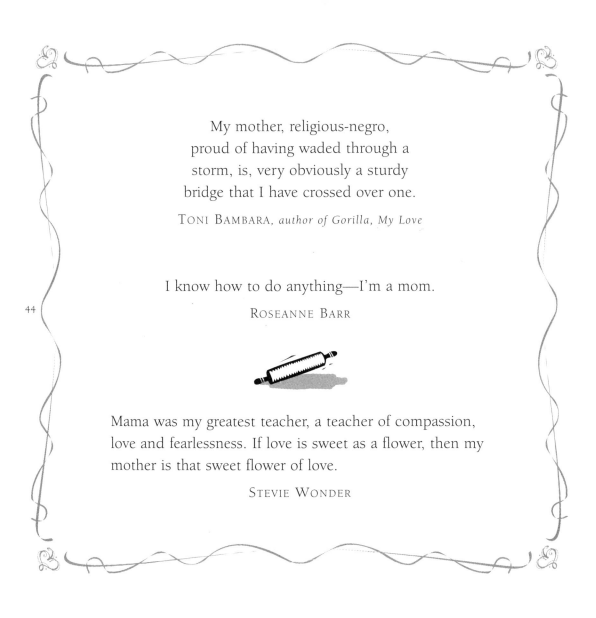

Mama was my greatest teacher, a teacher of compassion,
love and fearlessness. If love is sweet as a flower, then my
mother is that sweet flower of love.

STEVIE WONDER

It is said that life begins when the fetus
can exist apart from its mother. By definition,
many people in Hollywood are legally dead.

JAY LENO

On the bus back home, Ma began rambling on about
what being a girl had been like for her—how if she could
have changed one thing about herself, it would be her
shyness…"So when Tony came along and started calling
me on the telephone, showing me all of his attention,
well, I just couldn't—"

"Does any of this have a point?" I sighed.
"He was supposed to tell you. That was the purpose of
the whole week. Your father wants a divorce."

WALLY LAMB, *She's Come Undone*

Mother tells me "Happy dreams!" and
takes away the light,
An' leaves me lyin' all alone an' seein'
things at night.

EUGENE FIELD, Seein' Things

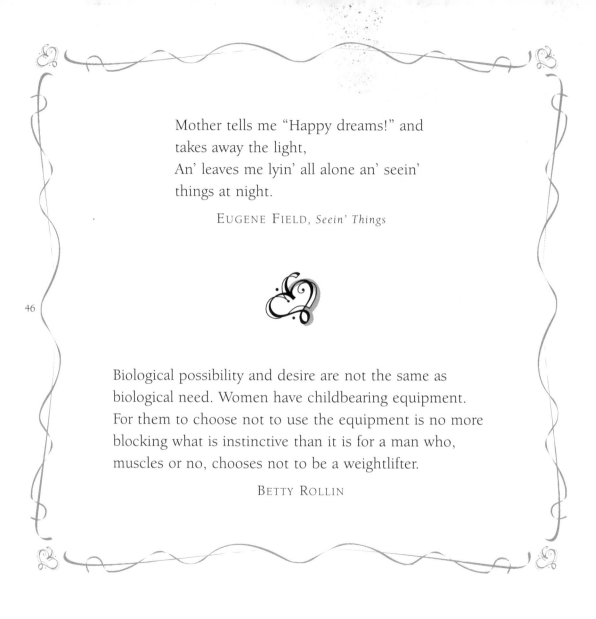

Biological possibility and desire are not the same as
biological need. Women have childbearing equipment.
For them to choose not to use the equipment is no more
blocking what is instinctive than it is for a man who,
muscles or no, chooses not to be a weightlifter.

BETTY ROLLIN

As is the mother, so is her daughter.

Ezekiel 1:44

And it came to me, and I knew what I had to have before
my soul would rest. I wanted to belong—to my mother.
And in return—I wanted my mother to belong to me.

Gloria Vanderbilt

In virtue alone is happiness...never was an existence
upon earth more blessed than my mother's.

John Quincy Adams

Children are what the mothers are.
No fondest father's fondest care
Can fashion so the infant heart.

WALTER SAVAGE LANDOR, *Children*

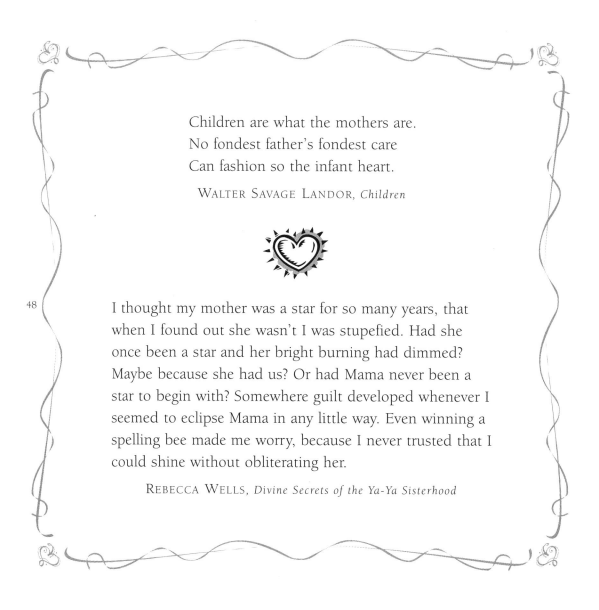

I thought my mother was a star for so many years, that
when I found out she wasn't I was stupefied. Had she
once been a star and her bright burning had dimmed?
Maybe because she had us? Or had Mama never been a
star to begin with? Somewhere guilt developed whenever I
seemed to eclipse Mama in any little way. Even winning a
spelling bee made me worry, because I never trusted that I
could shine without obliterating her.

REBECCA WELLS, *Divine Secrets of the Ya-Ya Sisterhood*

My mom got me a Davy Crockett t-shirt, which I wore for about 400 days in a row. I cannot remember any of the sonnets of Shakespeare, but I can remember several verses of "The Ballad of Davy Crockett..."

DAVE BARRY

The mother's face and voice are the first conscious objects as the infant soul unfolds, and she soon comes to stand in the very place of God to her child.

GRANVILLE STANLEY HALL, *Poet*

James James
Morrison Morrison
Weatherby George Dupree
Took great
Care of his Mother
Though he was only three.
James James
Said to his Mother,
"Mother ," he said, said he:
"You must never go down to the end
of the town, if you don't go down with me."

A. A. MILNE, *When We Were Very Young*

Mother set facing the front of the train,
as it makes her giddy to ride backwards.
I set facing her, which does not affect me.

RING LARDNER, *The Golden Honeymoon*

Homer: You couldn't fool your mother on your
most foolingist day of your life, even if you had an
electrified fooling machine.

HOMER, *The Simpsons*

If I was damned of body and soul,
I know whose prayers would make me whole,
Mother o'mine, O mother o' mine.

RUDYARD KIPLING

When I was about six years old, I developed an allergy to my favorite stuffed animal, a small gray elephant I had named Bar Bar (thinking that was the name of the famous story book elephant). One morning when I came back from breakfast, I couldn't find him anywhere. I looked and looked, but he had gone. I cried. I couldn't understand.

Mother, of course, had taken him while I was out of the room. She told me he must have had to go somewhere, and I believed her. It was a small consolation.

That night, right before dinner, she spotted a letter on the windowsill of the dining room. It was addressed to me. We lived on the fourth floor of a brick apartment building. How could a letter just appear on the window sill?

She helped me read it. It was from Bar Bar. He

wrote that he had had to go home to take care of his nephews. Their parents had suddenly had to take a long trip. He was the only one who could fill their place. I believed this. But I still didn't understand how the letter had reached the dining room. Mother told me that Sammy Squirrel had delivered it. He was a character in a children's book she had written before I was born. That made sense too.

Every few days for months after that, a letter from Bar Bar would appear on the windowsill. I never saw Sammy Squirrel deliver them. I never saw my mother write them. They were a lovely gift that made my loss bearable. Later that year, she did an oil painting of my favorite doll and in the corner of that picture is another picture - of Bar Bar. Thus, I have his image still, these many years later.

HONOR, AGE 54.

Happy he
With such a mother! faith in womankind
Beats with his blood, and trust in all things high
Comes easy to him; and tho' he trip and fall,
He shall not blind his soul with clay.

ALFRED LORD TENNYSON

One of the very few reasons I had any respect for my
mother when I was 13 was because she would reach into
the sink with her bare hands—BARE HANDS—and pick
up that lethal gunk and drop it into the garbage. To top
that, I saw her reach into the wet garbage bag and fish
around in there looking for a lost teaspoon. BARE
HANDED—a kind of mad courage.

ROBERT FULGHUM

Papa put into my hands a little packet of letters and papers telling me that they were mamma's, and that I might read them. I did read them, in a frame of mind I cannot describe. The papers were yellow with time, all having been written before I was born. It was strange now to peruse for the first time, the records of a mind whence my own sprang: and most strange, and at once sad and sweet, to find that a mind of a truly fine, pure and elevated order...There is a rectitude, a refinement, a constancy, a modesty, a sense of gentleness about them that is indescribable. I wish she had lived and that I had known her.

CHARLOTTE BRONTE, *letter to a friend*

As I look at my daughters...I am astounded at what they accomplish. They are better mothers than I was and they are the admitted equals of their husbands in intelligence and initiative. They go out to work or they study; they write or they teach; they weave or paint or play in musical groups.... Sometimes they do several of those things at once.

ANNE MORROW LINDBERGH, *Gifts from the Sea*

I don't recall [her] ever griping a lot. She's a strong lady. She wasn't a griper, and they always kind of made do—positive attitude.

CLINT EASTWOOD

Mom's are the spoonful of sugar that
helps the medicine go down.

DEBORAH, AGE 17

A mother is the truest friend we have, when trials,
heavy and sudden, fall upon us; when adversity takes
the place of prosperity; when friends who rejoice with
us in our sunshine, desert us when troubles thicken around us,
still will she cling to us, and endeavor by her kind precepts
and counsels to dissipate the clouds of darkness, and cause
peace to return to our hearts.

WASHINGTON IRVING

One moment a woman is pregnant and
the next she is a mother, an instant novitiate
in that secret society whose member
roll is as long as time itself.

MOLLY MCKAUGHAN, *The Biological Clock*

Who ran to help me when I fell,
And would some pretty story tell,
Or kiss the place to make it well?
My mother.

ANN TAYLOR *Poet*

My mother, for instance, thought—or, rather, knew—that it was dangerous to drive an automobile without gasoline...Her greatest dread, however, was the Victrola....She had an idea that the Victrola might blow up. It alarmed her, rather than reassured her, to explain that the phonograph was run neither by gasoline nor by electricity. She could only suppose that it was propelled by some newfangled and untested apparatus which was likely to let go at any minute, making us all the victims and martyrs of the wild-eyed Edison's dangerous experiments.

JAMES THURBER, *My Life and Hard Times*

59

I never did say that you can't be a nice guy and win.
I said that if I was playing third base and my mother
rounded third with the winning run, I'd trip her up.

LEO DUROCHER

My mother always seemed to me
a fairy princess, a radiant being possessed
of limitless riches and power.

WINSTON CHURCHILL

Discipline is a symbol of caring to a
child...If you have never been hated by
your child, you have never been a parent.

BETTE DAVIS

What Rules The World

They say that man is mighty;
He governs the land and sea,
He wields a might scepter
O'er lesser powers that be.
But a mightier power and stronger
Man from his throne has hurled,
For the hand that rocks the cradle
Is the hand that rules the world."

WILLIAM ROSS WALLACE.

She was so deeply imbedded in my consciousness that for
the first year of school I seem to have believed that each
of my teachers was my mother in disguise.

PHILIP ROTH, *Portnoy's Complaint*

There is nothing more thrilling in this world,
I think, than having a child that is yours,
and yet is mysteriously a stranger.

AGATHA CHRISTIE

One of these days, you'll shout, "Why don't you kids
grow up and act your age!" And they will....No more
plastic tablecloths stained with spaghetti...No more
sand in the sheets...A lipstick with a point on it...No
PTA meetings. No car pools. No blaring radios. No one
washing her hair at 11 o'clock at night. Having your
own roll of Scotch tape....

ERMA BOMBECK

...Ma landed a job as a tollbooth collector on the Newport Bridge...Her hair looked even blonder set against her khaki uniform. ...Within a week she had her first date. "He seems like a sweetheart," she said. "Hands me a Hershey's kiss with his money every morning. Take a chance, I told myself."

WALLY LAMB, *She's Come Undone*

Do not join encounter groups. If you enjoy being made to feel inadequate, call your mother.

LIZ SMITH

My mother has always been unhappy with what I do. She would rather I do something nicer, like be a bricklayer.

MICK JAGGER

No one but she could have brought about unity, even harmony, in a family of such strikingly varied personalities. She was the acknowledged head of the household.

SVETLANA ALLILUYEVA, *Stalin's daughter, about her mother*

With a mother of different mental caliber
I would probably have turned out badly.

THOMAS ALVA EDISON

One fine day... as my mother was putting the bread in the oven, I went up to her and taking her by her flour-smeared elbow I said to her, "Mama...I want to be a painter." ...My mother's love for me was so great that I have worked hard to justify it.

MARC CHAGALL